KING OF RAGTIME

The Story of Scott Joplin

STEPHEN COSTANZA

Atheneum Books for Young Readers
New York London Toronto Sydney New Delhi

ATHENEUM BOOKS FOR YOUNG READERS

An imprint of Simon & Schuster Children's Publishing Division

1230 Avenue of the Americas, New York, New York 10020

© 2021 by Stephen Costanza

Book design by Greg Stadnyk © 2021 by Simon & Schuster, Inc.

For information about special discounts for bulk purchases, please contact Simon & Schuster Special Sales at 1-866-506-1949 or business@simonandschuster.com.

The Simon & Schuster Speakers Bureau can bring authors to your live event. For more information or to book an event, contact the Simon & Schuster Speakers Bureau at 1-866-248-3049 or visit our website at www.simonspeakers.com.

The text for this book was set in New Caledonia.

The illustrations for this book were rendered in gouache, wax pastel, and collage.

Manufactured in China

1121 SCP

2 4 6 8 10 9 7 5 3

Library of Congress Cataloging-in-Publication Data

Names: Costanza, Stephen, author.

Title: King of ragtime: the story of Scott Joplin / by Stephen Costanza.

Description: First edition. | New York : Atheneum Books for Young Readers, [2021] |

Includes bibliographical references and index. Identifiers: LCCN 2018015146 (print) |

LCCN 2018016057 (eBook) |

ISBN 9781534410374 (eBook) | ISBN 9781534410367 (hardcover : alk. paper)

Subjects: LCSH: Joplin, Scott, 1868–1917—Juvenile literature. | Composers—

United States—Biography—Juvenile literature.

Classification: LCC ML3930.J66 (eBook) | LCC ML3930.J66 C67 2021 (print) |

DDC 780.92 [B]—dc23

LC record available at https://lccn.loc.gov/2018015146

Special thanks to Reka Simonsen, Claire Easton, Lori Nowicki,
Ashley Bryan, Joe Costanza, Eva Hopkins, Glenn Jenks,
Shirley Kline, Charles Pace, John Reed-Torres, Wayne Marshall,
Edward A. Berlin, and Aaron Robinson.

To my friend and mentor, Ashley Bryan,
who inspired me to keep marching onward

In the valley of the Red River,
  where the soil was as rich
  as most folks were poor,
four states sat side by side
like colors on a quilt
sewn from cotton picked
by black hands, brown hands,
tired and worn—but oh!
How they clapped at night,
as voices lifted to the stars.

These were the people newly free.
Turning to music for solace and celebration,
they sang spirituals,
and ring shouts,
and hollers on "Juneteenth," the nineteenth of June,
when slavery in Texas ended for good.

Under a canopy of red maple leaves,
a hymn swayed in the breeze—
sweet, like sugar cane.
Florence could see
her son's eyes light up when she sang.

Scott, the son of a man
who had been enslaved,
would someday make America dance.
They'd call him a king: the King of Ragtime.

SCOTT

Scott grew halfway high to a sunflower.
He hardly spoke above a whisper,
preferring to listen to the sounds around him.

Buzzz-zuzzz! hummed the wasp's nest.
Chhhh-chhhipp! chimed the cicadas.
Rrrrrrummm-bum-bum! grumbled the thundercloud; or no . . .
Was that a train?

And those old work songs,
how they'd lift his hands and feet
while he was shucking corn
or carrying buckets of water
heavier than himself.

In Scott's home, music flowed like the great river itself.
His father, Giles, fiddled,
His mother, Florence, plucked the banjo and sang,
while Monroe, Robert, Ossie, and William
played guitar, box fiddle, spoons, and fiddle.
Baby Myrtle helped with the spoons,
and Scott played the cornet.
He learned the pieces his father had played in the big house,
like schottisches, polkas, and waltzes.
Music filled the air like a breeze from Alabama.

RED RIVER VALLEY

Times were tough, and money was scarce.
Giles found work laying tracks for the
Texas & Pacific Railway for a dollar a day.

Scott and his family traveled north,
where a patch of Texas,
a scrap of Arkansas,
and a stripe of Louisiana
were all sewn into one town: Texarkana.

Florence worked as a housemaid for a wealthy white family and brought Scott along to help with the cleaning and laundry.

In the corner sat a piano,
a "square grand" made of dark cherry wood,
and eighty-eight mother-of-pearl keys waiting to be tickled.

PLINK!

PLoNK!

PLoNK!

PLINK!

Scott's dustcloth lightly wiped the keys. . . .
Plink plllink . . . plink!
He begged his mother to let him play it.

Plink plllink . . . plonk!
His heart skipped a beat
when each finger pressed
one key, then two.
Pling! PLANG!

That night, Scott's fingers
were still wiggling
when he should have been
fast asleep.

The next day, when his chores were done,
Scott raced to the piano
and felt the smooth keys dance beneath his fingers.

He followed the beat of his mother's broom,
and plucked out a lullaby she used to sing.

Swoosh-SWOOSH, *swoosh-SWISH!*
A duet filled the room,
a two-step for broom and piano.

He made up a ditty for dusting;
the day after, a waltz for washing.
He soon made up a tune for every chore.

A seed was planted and took root.
Florence knew a talent like Scott's had to be nurtured.

Florence and Giles scrimped and saved,
searching Texarkana for a piano,
but in the young town
a piano was as rare as a two-headed cat.

Then one day they saw a notice.

It was a dusty old thing
and out of tune in every string,
but when Julius Weiss heard Scott play,
he offered to give him piano lessons
if Florence did his housework.

The kindly man showed Scott everything about a piano:
scales, fingering, harmony, and dynamics.
Mr. Weiss taught him the popular tunes of the day:
ballads by Foster, marches by Sousa,
and arias from famous operas—
songs of wizards, princes, and dragons—
music that sent shivers down Scott's spine.

As soon as Scott finished learning one piece,
he'd get busy on another.
Whenever he got stuck,
he stayed up late and practiced
until he got it just right.

Most of all, he loved composing his own music.
He'd patch in a riff from a work song,
a thread of gospel here, a string of ring shout there—
sewing together new tunes
to play for his mother the next day.

All of Scott's neighbors began talking about the quiet kid who made a piano laugh out loud.

He played at church socials, dances, and his favorite event of all, the annual Juneteenth celebration.

Scott didn't need to play anyone else's music.
He simply played from his heart,
and it was beautiful.

"Scott," said Giles, "the piano's all well and good,
but it's not anything to hang your hopes on.
You'll be a man soon, and a man's work
is on the railroad."

On the one hand, his father was right.
The railroad offered steady work
for a young African American man
when so few opportunities existed.

But music was bubbling inside him,
and courage came on like a head of steam.
Scott needed to get on that train
and see what was at the end of the line.

Black people weren't allowed to sit with white people,
so Scott sat in the back of the train
with the other Black people searching
for opportunity and a new life.

Through hills, sand, and hot stone,
Scott rattled and rolled on that train—
the **_bumpa-bump!_** rhythms in his left hand,
the **_clickety-clackety!_** in his right.

Scott knew he could make a living with music, but how?

He soon found work playing the piano in saloons and honky-tonks all along the Mississippi Valley.

No one noticed the quiet young man
until he started making up his own tunes—
an **OOM-pah! OOM-pah!** in the left hand,
the ***plinkety-PLONK!*** in the right.

Toes tapped to the snappy rhythms.
Who knew a piano could roar like a train
or sing like a nightingale?

It was the sound of Scott dreaming of a respectable career,
not one confined to saloons.

In 1893, Scott arrived in Chicago,
where the World's Fair was in full swing.
He was dazzled by the electric lights
and the world's first Ferris wheel.
But most of all, there was MUSIC.

Black pianists weren't allowed to play at the fair,
but in the nearby cafés
a red-hot piano sound filled the air.

The left hand kept the beat, ***OOM-pah, OOM-pah!***
The right hand soared, free as a bird;
syncopated, agitated, bodacious, and proud!
Folks pranced and danced to a new music called . . .

What could Scott do
with all that music
buzzing in his brain?

The music went
round and round
in his head.

Scott took the train to Sedalia, Missouri, where he got work as a piano teacher, and as a pianist at the Maple Leaf Club. He also attended the George R. Smith College for Negroes, where he learned to put his ideas on paper.

Scott wrote two songs: a waltz, and an **OOM-pah!** march in the popular style of the day. But it wasn't the music he heard in his soul.

This time he would write a piece as much fun to listen to as it would be to play.

SEDALIA, MO.

He took the **OOM-pah! OOM-pah!** in the left hand, the *syncopated* rhythms in the right, and called it "Maple Leaf Rag," after the club where he played.

Something told Scott it was special, but the publishers
turned him down. **"Much too difficult,"** they said.

But Scott wasn't about to give up. He got an idea.
He played the piece for music publisher John Stark,
while a group of kids danced and wiggled to the catchy tune.

It was impossible to sit still!

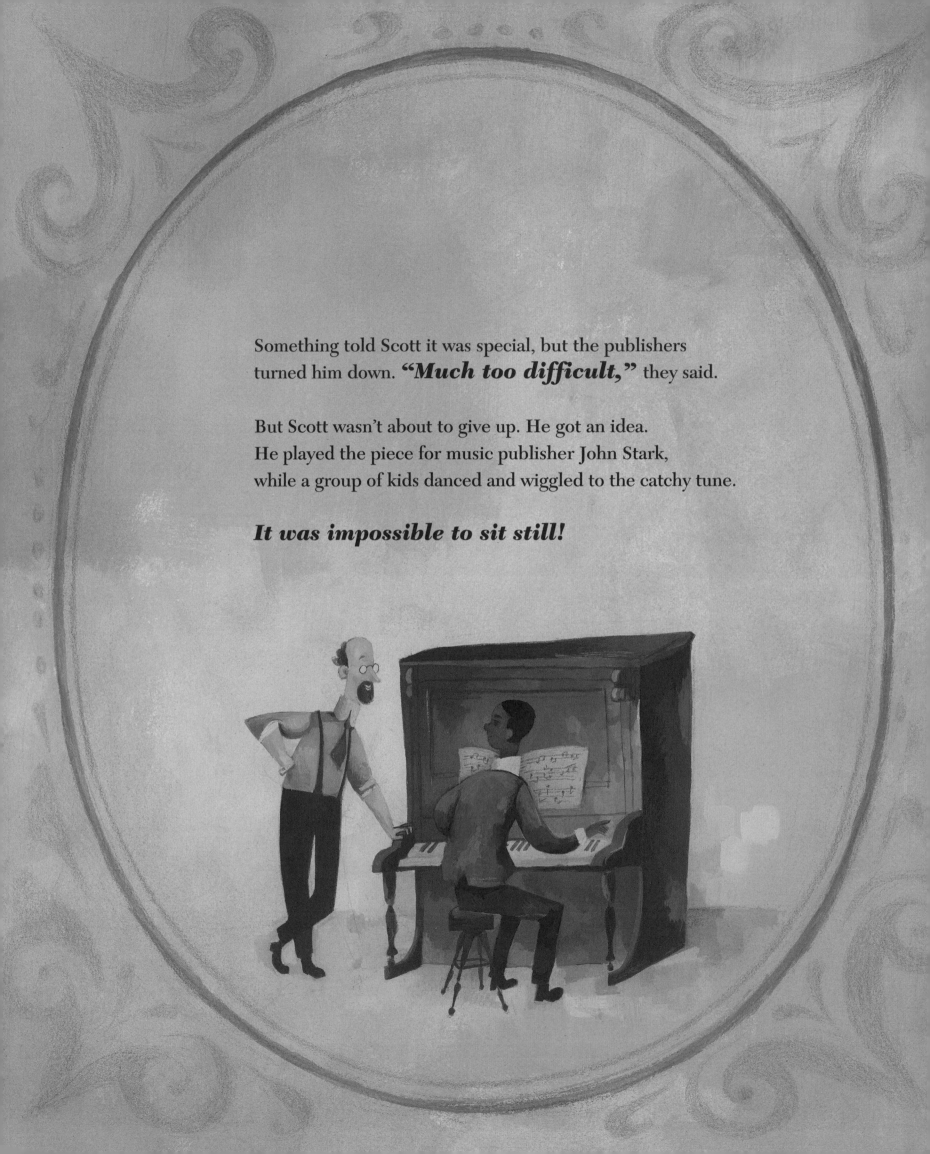

At last John Stark said the words Scott longed to hear: **They had a deal, and a contract.**

It was an uncommon arrangement for an unknown composer, especially one who was African American.

But Scott believed in his music, and John Stark was willing to take a chance.

For the first year, sales were slow,
but by the autumn of 1900,
the "Maple Leaf Rag" was heard
in every parlor, dance hall, and theater.

This ragtime hit
had taken the nation by storm.

To the Maple Leaf Club.
MAPLE LEAF RAG.
By King of Ragtime writers Scott Joplin.
Scott Joplin
Published by
STARK & SON
ST. LOUIS, MO.

A new cover to the sheet music was printed,
this time with Scott's photograph
and the proud proclamation:
"By King of Ragtime writers, Scott Joplin."

Soon Scott's name was known throughout the land.
With the success of the "Maple Leaf Rag,"
he was able to leave the world of saloons behind
and focus on what he loved most of all: writing music.

Scott went on to write many more ragtime pieces,
taking the **OOM-pah!** in his left hand
and the raggedy-jaggedy syncopations in his right.

He sat down at the piano
and, with both hands,
created a new music,
an American music
like the country itself—
a patchwork of sounds
and colors.

NONPAREIL
THE RAGTIME DANCE
TREEMONISHA
BETHENA
ROSE LEAF RAG
WALL ST. RAG
LEOLA
PARAGON RAG
EUPHONIC SOUNDS
THE SYCAMORE
FIG LEAF RAG
THE EASY WINNERS
WEEPING WILLOW
THE CASCADES
GLADIOLUS RAG

Author's Note

On August 10, 1899, a quiet, reserved, little-known composer in Sedalia, Missouri, walked across town with a new piece for piano under his arm. The music was bright, danceable, and red-hot, with thumping octaves for the left hand, and jittery syncopations for the right. He sold the piece to a local publisher, and while not an immediate hit, the music eventually took hold. By 1904, sales of the "Maple Leaf Rag" put the small-town publisher on the map and rocketed the young African American composer to international fame. His name was Scott Joplin, and he was crowned "the King of Ragtime Writers."

Ragtime was an American dance music that, from 1897 to 1917, heralded the new century with its streetcar sounds and street-smart vibe. It touched off a musical revolution, the first great impact of Black culture on the dominant white middle-class culture of America. There were ragtime songs and ragtime band arrangements, but this jubilant new music found its fullest expression on the piano. At a time when pianos were as common in American homes as the kitchen sink, this fusion of African and European idioms created a heady, intoxicating brew—a full-bodied piano sound that made people want to move their feet.

But not everyone was dancing. The American Federation of Musicians ordered its members to desist from playing ragtime, declaring, "The musicians know what is good, and if the people don't, we will have to teach them." Others were equally insulting, calling the music "hateful" and "degenerate," not least because of its association with African Americans. But insults and racism could not prevent a glittering array of rag composers, Black and white, from finding publishers who recognized their extraordinary talent. Far and away the leader of these composers was the quiet man from Texas, Scott Joplin.

When Joplin's "Maple Leaf Rag" first appeared, it set the gold standard for ragtime composition. Even today it stands out, with its rhythmic intensity and irrepressible forward drive. But with the benefit of hindsight, we can see how this early work only hinted at the full extent of Joplin's genius.

In Scott Joplin's hands, the rag was conceived as a complete and self-sufficient musical form in itself. While a handful of gifted contemporaries followed in his footsteps, none could approach the structural elegance, melodic inventiveness, and emotional depth that characterized his major works. Nor would any other rag composer match

his ambitions for the music—ambitions that led to the composition of two operas, a ballet, and other works that squarely challenged the reputation of rag as lowbrow. As an African American living during the time of jim crow—a strictly enforced racist system of racial segregation and repression of Black people—Joplin faced discrimination at every turn. Nevertheless, he worked mightily to create an art that would serve as a powerful and dignified voice for his people.

Yet success eluded the King of Ragtime Writers; not only his large-scale works but even his finest piano rags were largely overlooked. As more and more composers flooded the market with novelty rags, piano players reciprocated with dizzy-fingered performances of speed and showmanship. Joplin's response was unequivocal. He inserted a tempo warning at the top of many of his scores: "Do not play this piece fast. It is never right to play ragtime fast."

But the times *were* moving fast. By 1917, when America entered World War I, the ragtime era had all but faded, and when Joplin departed this world that same year, his music seemed to vanish with him. Only the "Maple Leaf Rag" entered the repertoire of restless musicians from New Orleans to Chicago to New York, those who tilled the fertile soil of ragtime and blues, and harvested the first fruits of a new music called jazz.

America may have largely forgotten Joplin's musical genius during the jazz age and swing era, but the "Maple Leaf Rag" kept his spirit alive, becoming a repertoire standard in the true sense, an eternal flame for the onetime King of Ragtime Writers. Then, sometime in the late 1940s, interest in the man and his music started to resurface, as ragtime increasingly became recognized as a distinct genre, rather than merely a subset of traditional jazz.

By the 1970s, the rediscovery of Scott Joplin and his music was in full swing, and he was at long last enshrined as a major American composer. Some sixty-odd years after the debut of his opera *Treemonisha*, the work was successfully revived, recorded, and its composer posthumously awarded a Pulitzer Prize. His music was seemingly everywhere—the movies, TV, radio—and on the eager fingertips of kids taking piano lessons, like myself. Sales of his recordings reached rock-star levels, but the LP *Piano Rags by Scott Joplin*, performed by pianist Joshua Rifkin, stopped me in my tracks. It's an album of eight rags spanning Joplin's career, and I listened to each piece as if turning a gemstone over and over in my hands.

The beauty and mystery of this music invited questions. I needed to know more about its creator. Who was this young Texan, from the first generation of African Americans born after Emancipation? Who was this sharecropper's son who rose from obscurity to international recognition? Who was this man in the grainy photographs—by all accounts serious and soft-spoken, and who rarely smiled—who made the piano not only sing but laugh out loud? As I dived headfirst into the music, my piano teacher Mrs. Field patiently sat through every Joplin rag I played, or attempted to play, even when I was supposed to be practicing Schubert.

For a man whose music is now so well known, we know precious little of Scott Joplin himself. He left behind few possessions, little money, and no diaries or letters. What remains is his music. In this book I have attempted to piece together a picture of Joplin's early life, taken from the bits of information we do have.

Scott Joplin was born in 1867 or 1868,

in what is now Cass County in north Texas. His father, the formerly enslaved Giles Joplin, worked as a laborer. His mother, Florence Givens Joplin, was born free in Kentucky. When Scott was about seven years old, the family moved to Texarkana, an up-and-coming railroad town on the Texas-Arkansas border. In the post–Civil War era, the cruel breath of slavery and the failed plan of Reconstruction still hung in the air. In those early days of Texarkana there were no schools, for Blacks or whites. At least some of the Joplin children were tutored, for their parents were anxious that they learn to read and write.

The Joplin children were also learning about music. Giles played the violin, having performed for dances and entertainments in the "Big House," the name given to the enslaver's home in the days before the Emancipation Proclamation. Florence sang and played the banjo, while Scott's sisters and brothers rounded out the musical scene. But even among his talented siblings, Scott stood out.

In Black Texarkana, music was as integral a part of life as breathing, and Scott's childhood was filled with the music of his people. There were hymns and spirituals, work songs and chants; he heard melodies passed down from generation to generation, and sang in rooms that came alive with the clapping of hands and the tapping of feet. This was the ring shout, first observed in America among enslaved African people in the 1700s as a holy dance. A singer called out the leading lines of a song, clappers sang the response, a stickman controlled the rhythm and pace by banging a stick or broom against the floor, while the singers formed a circle and moved, counterclockwise, to the beat. Singing, percussion, and movement all came together in one glorious communal expression of hope, resilience, and love.

But he also absorbed the music that spun off his father's fiddle: the European modes of music such as gavottes, polkas, waltzes, and reels. The western European musical forms mingled freely with the rhythms and "blue" notes so strongly rooted in the African tradition, shaping Scott's conception of music and his creation of beautiful sounds.

A turning point came sometime in the early 1880s, when Giles left the family. Florence, having to take care of their six children, found domestic work in Texarkana's white-owned homes, and she often brought Scott along. At one house belonging to the Cook family, she obtained permission for young Scott to play their piano as she went about her chores. At the Cooks', Scott's fingers brushed the smooth keys for the first time.

Scott's musical gifts found free expression on the square grand piano, and before long he was teaching himself how to play. Despite her limited resources, Florence managed to pull enough money together to purchase a piano for Scott. She also arranged for him to study with several local music teachers.

Among them was a German immigrant named Julius Weiss. Legend has it that Weiss gave lessons to Scott in exchange for housework from Florence, so impressed was he by the young boy's talent. And Joplin most certainly impressed his teacher, with his ear for harmony and gift for improvisation. Lessons with Julius Weiss opened up new worlds for him—piano technique, music theory, musical theater, and opera—that would remain with Scott Joplin for the rest of his life.

Perhaps Scott's greatest teacher, however, was his mother, Florence. She saw the glint in her son's eyes when the house filled with music; she witnessed first-hand his captivation with the piano at the Cooks'. Her example of courage and self-sufficiency in the face of adversity surely left its mark on him, and years later, Joplin must have had her in mind when creating the heroine in his opera *Treemonisha*.

By his teens, Scott was playing at churches, clubs, and social gatherings in the border area of Texas and Arkansas, having become a kind of celebrity in the Black community. A window to that world comes to us from Zenobia Campbell, a Texarkana resident from those days. She remembered, "He did not have to play anyone else's music. He made up his own, and it was beautiful; he just got his music out of the air." Her words inspired the Juneteenth scene in this book.

At some point in the mid-1880s Scott moved to Saint Louis and earned a living as a pianist in saloons and dance halls called honky-tonks, and with a band. But he also traveled widely, rubbing shoulders with other musicians, sharing ideas with like-minded pianists who stood at the forefront of an exciting new way of playing. His visit to the Chicago World's Fair in 1893 may have been especially influential. Ragtime music had yet to be published but apparently was widely played at the fair, albeit on the outskirts of the fairgrounds. Black musicians were not permitted to play in the centrally located venues, but that didn't stop their music from reaching a wide and captivated audience.

In 1894, Joplin settled in Sedalia, Missouri, a prosperous city with a thriving music scene. Scott felt at home in the community: He tutored pianists, helped form a baseball team, organized various events and musicales, and sang second tenor and toured with the Texas Medley Quartet. But there was music inside him, *his* music, and he had to set it free. He studied harmony and composition at the George R. Smith College, and after a small collection of published compositions, began writing the "Maple Leaf Rag," the piece that would soon establish him as King of Ragtime Writers.

But Joplin didn't wait for fame to arrive. Not only did he get busy writing more rags, he immediately turned his attention to musical theater with the ballet *The Ragtime Dance*; following it a few years later with *A Guest of Honor*, his first opera. In the midst of these genre-breaking excursions into other musical forms, the rags grew in scope, complexity, and emotional intensity. Joplin was not only writing music that had people dancing, but also composing deeply reflective, poignant works, all the while experiencing the many obstacles that a Black man was forced to endure in America. His response was a gift for all time; these dances without dancers, America's own songs without words.

I invite you to take Scott Joplin's music into your own hands. Listening to his pieces fosters lasting memories; to play them brings him into your soul. What's more, the music simply feels good under the fingers—the parlor waltz refinement of "Bethena," the astonishing anticipation of boogie-woogie in "Pine Apple Rag," the *misterioso* passages of "Leola," the miniature theater-piece that is "Wall St. Rag," the magnetic "Magnetic Rag," and of course, the evergreen "Maple Leaf Rag." These and other gems await in Scott Joplin's constellation, an essential part of our American musical fabric.

Recommended Listening

Scott Joplin Piano Rags
Joshua Rifkin, piano
Nonesuch B000005IYF

Euphonic Sounds
Reginald R. Robinson, piano
Delmark

Scott Joplin: The Complete Rags, Waltzes and Marches
William Appling, piano
CD Baby

Treemonisha
Houston Grand Opera conducted by Günter Schuller
Deutsche Grammaphon B000OSQ6S8

The World of Scott Joplin
Max Morath, piano
Vanguard B000000EDN

The Red Back Book
New England Conservatory Ragtime Ensemble conducted by Günter Schuller
Angel Records B00J89X0C4

Bibliography

Bankston, John. *The Life and Times of Scott Joplin*. Hockessin: Mitchell Lane Publishing, Inc. 2004.

Berlin, Edward A. *King of Ragtime: Scott Joplin and His Era*. 2nd ed. New York: Oxford University Press, 2016.

Curtis, Susan. *Dancing to a Black Man's Tune: A Life of Scott Joplin*. Columbia: University of Missouri Press, 2004.

Foner, Eric. *A Short History of Reconstruction*. Updated edition. New York: Harper Perennial, 2015.

Gioia, Ted. *The History of Jazz*. 2nd ed. New York: Oxford University Press, 2011.

Hamilton, Marybeth. *In Search of the Blues*. New York: Basic Books, 2008.

Haskins, James. *Scott Joplin: The Man Who Made Ragtime*. With Kathleen Benson. London: Robson Books, 1979.

Schafer, William J., and Johannes Riedel. *The Art of Ragtime: Form and Meaning of an Original Black American Art*. With assistance from Michael Polad and Richard Thompson. New York: DaCapo Press, Inc.

Joplin, Scott. *The Collected Works of Scott Joplin* 2 vols., 2nd ed., edited by Vera Brodsky Lawrence. New York: New York Public Library, 1971.